PSHE & Citizenship In Action

Year 4

Godfrey Hall

© 2004 Folens Limited, on behalf of the author

United Kingdom: Folens Publishers, Apex Business Centre, Boscombe Road, Dunstable, LU5 4RL
Email: folens@folens.com

Ireland: Folens Publishers, Greenhills Road, Tallaght, Dublin 24
Email: info@folens.ie

Poland: JUKA, ul. Renesansowa 38, Warsaw 01-905

Folens allows photocopying of pages marked 'copiable page' for educational use, providing that this use is within the confines of the purchasing institution. Copiable pages should not be declared in any return in respect of any photocopying licence.

Folens books are protected by international copyright laws. All rights are reserved. The copyright of all materials in this publication, except where otherwise stated, remains the property of the publisher and the author. No part of this publication may be reproduced, stored in a retrieval system, or transmitted, in any form or by any means, for whatever purpose, without the written permission of Folens Limited.

Godfrey Hall hereby asserts his moral right to be identified as the author of this work in accordance with the Copyright, Designs and Patents Act 1988.

Editor: Melanie Gray
Layout artist: Suzanne Ward
Illustrations: Mark Stacey
Cover design: Martin Cross

First published 2004 by Folens Limited.

Every effort has been made to contact copyright holders of material used in this book. If any copyright holder has been overlooked, we shall be pleased to make any necessary arrangements.

British Library Cataloguing in Publication Data. A catalogue record for this publication is available from the British Library.

ISBN 1 84303 634 7

Contents

Series introduction — 4

Unit 1 Communication — 5
Worksheet 1 Sending a message — 6
Worksheet 2 Listen carefully — 7
Worksheet 3 How do we feel? — 8

Unit 2 Working together — 9
Worksheet 4 Working in a group — 10
Worksheet 5 Playground activities — 11
Worksheet 6 Feedback — 12

Unit 3 Decisions — 13
Worksheet 7 Friendship — 14
Worksheet 8 Remember this — 15
Worksheet 9 Different audiences — 16

Unit 4 Animals — 17
Worksheet 10 Unwanted pets — 18
Worksheet 11 The RSPCA — 19
Worksheet 12 Owning a pet — 20

Unit 5 The police — 21
Worksheet 13 What do we do? — 22
Worksheet 14 Vandalism and damage — 23
Worksheet 15 Antisocial behaviour — 24

Unit 6 The world we live in — 25
Worksheet 16 International trade — 26
Worksheet 17 The global village — 27
Worksheet 18 City life — 28

Unit 7 Our school — 29
Worksheet 19 Creating a committee — 30
Worksheet 20 Working together — 31
Worksheet 21 What do you think? — 32

Unit 8 Rights — 33
Worksheet 22 A charter of rights — 34
Worksheet 23 What happens if things go wrong? — 35
Worksheet 24 Sorting out conflict — 36

Unit 9 Rules and laws — 37
Worksheet 25 Improving rules — 38
Worksheet 26 How old? — 39
Worksheet 27 Being the victim — 40

Unit 10 Respect — 41
Worksheet 28 Shoplifting — 42
Worksheet 29 Making changes — 43
Worksheet 30 Respecting your school — 44

Unit 11 Local democracy — 45
Worksheet 31 Our local council — 46
Worksheet 32 What do they do? — 47
Worksheet 33 Voting — 48

Unit 12 The media — 49
Worksheet 34 Headlines — 50
Worksheet 35 Sorting the news — 51
Worksheet 36 Soap operas — 52

Unit 13 At risk — 53
Worksheet 37 Fighting illness — 54
Worksheet 38 Taking a risk — 55
Worksheet 39 Safety on the road — 56

Unit 14 Drugs — 57
Worksheet 40 Why take drugs? — 58
Worksheet 41 Smoking — 59
Worksheet 42 The dangers of alcohol — 60

Unit 15 Bullying — 61
Worksheet 43 Being different — 62
Worksheet 44 Being confident — 63
Worksheet 45 Beating the bully — 64

Series introduction

This series has been designed to meet the needs of Key Stages 1 and 2. Prepared in conjunction with the QCA Schemes of Work for Citizenship, it also includes sections on personal, social and health education (PSHE).

Citizenship is a central issue in all schools, and a subject which is part and parcel of our everyday lives. Together with PSHE, it provides pupils with the knowledge, skills and understanding that are required for them to lead happy and confident lives.

It is also important that young people grow up to become not only responsible but active and informed citizens.

Issues covered in this series include:
- right and wrong
- rules and laws
- fairness
- healthy living
- being part of the community
- decision making
- conflict and cooperation.

The material and ideas in these books have been designed so that they can be used:
- as part of an ongoing programme
- as a springboard for further investigation
- to support existing schemes.

There are 15 units in each book. Each unit contains three sections, which focus on one issue and include a worksheet to help carry out that task. Each unit provides:
- background information
- learning objectives
- QCA and Curriculum links
- differentiated activities
- follow-up ideas
- three worksheets.

The worksheets have been provided so that they are flexible and can be adapted to the local needs of schools and individual teachers. The activities have also been designed so that they are cross-curricular.

In the later books, pupils are encouraged to work more and more with outside agencies, extending their knowledge of the subject on both a global and a national level.

Many of the activities throughout the series are excellent starting points for projects within the community as well as for links with other schools.

With the development of e-mail and the Internet, pupils are not only able to communicate with others throughout the world; they are also able to carry out intensive research into areas of interest. This allows schools to build partnerships with others. Pupils also have the chance to work closely with their peers. Working with others, investigating sustainable development and developing local and national strategies are all part of this process.

Citizenship and PSHE are important elements of the curriculum because they:
- encourage pupils to take a full part in the life of the school and the community
- provide pupils with the opportunity to become responsible citizens
- link schools with others elsewhere in the world
- provide the ingredients for a healthy lifestyle
- support and promote equal opportunity and respect
- provide a focus for school-based projects
- provide a chance to work on real-life issues
- increase pupils' decision-making opportunities.

 Communication

Background
This unit looks at the way in which we might deliver a message and the importance of effective communication using our voices in different ways. It also deals with effective listening and how we should take the needs and the feelings of the listener into account when talking to someone.

Learning Objectives
Activities in this unit will allow children to:
- develop as an effective communicator
- understand that you should also be a good listener
- take into consideration the feelings of the listener.

QCA/Curriculum links: QCA Unit 1 • Worksheet 1 links with English, Science and Design & Technology • Worksheet 2 links with English and Science • Worksheet 3 links with English.

ACTIVITIES

Worksheet 1 — Sending a message

Starting points: This worksheet concentrates on the importance of providing a clear and concise message. This can be demonstrated by asking the children to pass a verbal message down a line. A simple message can be given to the first child and then whispered along the line. If the children sit back to back, they will have to concentrate on using their voice rather than facial expressions.

Main activity: The children should read the sentences on the worksheet and write down one sentence to convey a clear and accurate message.

Simplified activity: Ask one child to give a command to another, once only. They then have to write down the command and pass it on to the next person, who also has to write it down. This should take place three or four times. Get the child at the end to read out the command. Is it the same as the one at the beginning?

Challenge: The children could consider what they can do to their voice to make the message clear.

Worksheet 2 — Listen carefully

Starting points: List some of the most important things you must do if you are given an important message, e.g. make sure you can hear the person clearly, ask them to repeat the message.

Main activity: The children should look at the four places on the worksheet. Ask them which place would be the best to give someone a message and why.

Simplified activity: The children could think about why it is important to listen carefully to a message.

Challenge: Ask the children to write a story about someone who gets a message wrong.

Worksheet 3 — How do we feel?

Starting points: Explain to the children that it is important to consider the feelings of the person you are talking to. If they are feeling sad for any reason, you should change the tone of your voice. Sometimes it might be better to tell them something later, when they are not upset or feeling unwell.

Main activity: The children should look at the drawings on the worksheet, read the messages below each person and decide which message(s) they would pass on and why.

Simplified activity: Ask the children how they might start a conversation with each of the people on the worksheet.

Challenge: Ask the children how they think they would react if you told them that (a) they had just won a holiday in Spain, and (b) their pet was ill.

Plenary
Talk about the importance of clear communication. Tell a story using the wrong expressions and voice, e.g. smile when something is sad. Discuss how what we do in a conversation is as important as what we say.

Worksheet 1

Sending a message

Read the sentences below. Write a one-line message to sum up each one.

1. Emily is having a party at 7.30 pm on Saturday to celebrate her birthday. She is inviting a group of friends to come along. There will be food, games and music. Emily will be ten years old. The party is to be held at her house.

   _____

2. The gang are going to the country on Sunday. They are going to be walking across fields and along muddy footpaths. They will be out all day. It is important that they bring wellington boots or a good strong pair of shoes.

   _____

3. Gemma's pet rabbit has been very ill. It was unwell on Thursday and did not eat any of the food it was given. It became weaker on Friday and unfortunately died on Saturday afternoon. Gemma was very fond of the rabbit, which she had kept as a pet for three years.

   _____

© Folens (copiable page) PSHE & Citizenship in Action: Year 4

Worksheet 2

Listen carefully

 **Look at the four drawings below. Which would be the best place to give someone a message? Explain why.**

A

B

C

D

I would choose place _____ because _____

_____

_____

Worksheet 3

How do we feel?

 Look at the pictures below. Which message would you pass on to these people? Explain why. You can choose more than one message for each person.

1. You have won £10.
2. Your pet is very ill.
3. You must go home now.

1. You have to see the teacher.
2. You must collect your lunch from your mum.
3. Your sister has been in an accident.

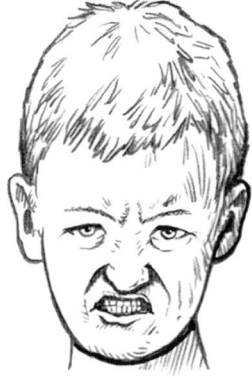

1. Beth says she doesn't like you.
2. You can come to tea with us.
3. Someone has just taken your coat home by mistake.

1. Playtime is over.
2. I can't find your bag.
3. Joe needs to borrow your pencil.

Working together

Background
This unit looks at the advantages and disadvantages of working in a group and then at how a group might work together on a new playground activity. Finally, the children have the opportunity to prepare their own questionnaire to find out what people think of the idea. This information can be fed back so that future work can be improved.

Learning Objectives
Activities in this unit will allow children to:
- develop their ability to work as a group
- understand why working as a group can sometimes be an advantage
- begin to assess their work and evaluate further group projects.

QCA/Curriculum links: QCA Unit 1 • Worksheet 4 links with English and Design & Technology • Worksheet 5 links with English, Science, Design & Technology and ICT • Worksheet 6 links with English.

ACTIVITIES

Worksheet 4 — Working in a group

Starting points: Divide the class into groups of four or five. Set them the task of making a paper aeroplane, and provide each group with a set of instructions. Ask the children to decide what each member of the group will do, e.g. one member could design different planes, one or two could test the designs, one could write out the instructions on how to make the most successful plane. Set a time limit for this activity.

Main activity: The children should complete the worksheet, showing in easy stages how the plane can be constructed.

Simplified activity: The children could make and fly the plane.

Challenge: Ask the children to discuss their designs and how they might be improved. This will help the groups appreciate the importance of constructive criticism.

Worksheet 5 — Playground activities

Starting points: In groups, carry out a survey of the kind of activities that take place during playtimes and consider how these might be extended.

Main activity: The children should fill in the questionnaire about the activities that take place during playtime.

Simplified activity: Ask the children to think about what other activities could take place in the playground. What things would need to be provided (e.g. balls, apparatus). Would providing these things cause any problems?

Challenge: The children could make a list of why the task might be easier if they work as a group.

Worksheet 6 — Feedback

Starting points: Discuss with the groups the importance of feedback. Ask the children to introduce some of their ideas at playtime. Ask each group to prepare a questionnaire that they could give to a random sample of children to find out what they think of the changes.

Main activity: The children should produce a questionnaire that can be used to get a cross-section of views from different children.

Simplified activity: Ask the children to write a list of six questions that could be asked in a possible survey to find out people's opinions of the changes.

Challenge: The children could produce a short report on their findings.

Plenary
Discuss what it has been like working as group. Would the children consider repeating this or do they prefer to work on their own? What other projects could they work on together? What are the differences between working as a group and as an individual? What makes a good group member?

Worksheet 4

Working in a group

Fill in this worksheet to show how your plane could be made.

Project: _____

Team members: _____

_____

_____

_____

_____

_____

Notes

_____
_____
_____
_____

Task

Worksheet 5

Playground activities

 **Fill in this worksheet about the kind of activities that take place during playtimes.**

1. What kind of activities go on at playtime?
   _____
   _____

2. What kind of games are played?
   _____
   _____

3. Is any special equipment needed? If so, what?
   _____
   _____

4. What kind of activities could be added?
   _____
   _____

5. What type of equipment would be needed for these new activities?
   _____
   _____

6. List some other possible suggestions for things to do.
   _____
   _____

7. What happens if it is wet at playtime?
   _____
   _____

Worksheet 6

Feedback

Write your own set of questions below.

1. _____

2. _____

3. _____

4. _____

5. _____

6. _____

3) Decisions

Background
This unit looks at the importance of friendship and how we can sometimes disagree with someone and still remain friends. The second part of the unit looks at adverts, particularly those we can remember, and goes on to examine how advertisers go about targeting different audiences.

Learning Objectives
Activities in this unit will allow children to:
- examine the meaning of friendship
- understand more clearly the reason behind advertising
- investigate how advertisers target certain audiences.

QCA/Curriculum links: QCA Unit 2 • Worksheet 7 links with English • Worksheet 8 links with English, ICT and Art & Design • Worksheet 9 links with English.

ACTIVITIES

Worksheet 7 — Friendship

Starting points: Talk about the meaning of the word 'friendship'. What makes a good friend? What might friends disagree about? How important is it to say sorry?

Main activity: The children should consider the situations on the worksheet. Which of the things might cause friends to fall out with each other?

Simplified activity: Ask the children to think about how they would make up with a friend after a disagreement.

Challenge: The children could write a list of things that they might do with their best friend.

Worksheet 8 — Remember this

Starting points: Explain to the children that advertisers use different methods to get us to remember their adverts and products. Talk about favourite TV adverts and why the children remember them.

Main activity: The children should look at the products and draw and write underneath anything they can remember from an advert they have seen for a similar product.

Simplified activity: Ask the children to collect some favourite adverts from newspapers and magazines.

Challenge: The children could look through local newspapers, choose a local company or shop and design an advert to promote one or more of their products.

Worksheet 9 — Different audiences

Starting points: Look at a selection of adverts in newspapers, magazines, the Internet and on TV. Discuss who the adverts might appeal to. What have the advertisers done to them to make them more appealing to certain people?

Main activity: The children should look at the adverts on the worksheet, writing down who they might appeal to and why.

Simplified activity: Ask the children to draw an advert for a toy that would appeal to a young audience.

Challenge: The children could choose a product and design three adverts for it. Each advert should appeal to a different audience.

Plenary
Ask the children to produce two adverts for assembly. Organise it so that the same product is shown in each advert, but is aimed at a different audience. Discuss why advertisers need to target certain things at different people. Talk about some of the adverts that appear on behalf of charities, e.g. the NSPCC, Cancer Care. What do advertisers do to get people's attention?

PSHE & Citizenship in Action: Year 4

Worksheet 7

Friendship

 **Friends don't always agree with each other. Look at the pictures below. Would you agree to do this? Explain why.**

Your friend asks you to drink some beer.

_____
_____
_____
_____

Your friend asks you to take a short cut across the railway line.

_____
_____
_____
_____

Your friend asks if they can cut your hair for you.

_____
_____
_____
_____

What could you do to make up with a friend?

_____
_____
_____

Worksheet 8

Remember this

 **Look at these products. Draw a scene from an advert advertising each product. Write down anything you can remember about the advert.**

 Toy

 Soap powder

 Car

Toilet paper

© Folens (copiable page) PSHE & Citizenship in Action: Year 4

Worksheet 9

Different audiences

Who do you think these adverts would appeal to? Explain why.

I think this advert would appeal to _____

because _____

I think this advert would appeal to _____

because _____

I think this advert would appeal to _____

because _____

I think this advert would appeal to _____

because _____

4 Animals

Background

This unit explores why people abandon their pets. It then goes on to to investigate the work of the RSPCA and finally there is a worksheet on the importance of pet ownership.

Learning Objectives

Activities in this unit will allow children to:
- discuss why people abandon pets
- examine the organisation of one charity
- explore the issues of being a pet owner.

QCA/Curriculum links: QCA Unit 3 • Worksheet 10 links with English and Science • Worksheet 11 links with English and History • Worksheet 12 links with English and Science.

ACTIVITIES

Worksheet 10 — Unwanted pets

Starting points: Discuss why some people buy a pet and then abandon it shortly afterwards. What are the reasons for this? Should people be allowed to do this? What is wrong with doing this?

Main activity: The children should make a list of some of the reasons why people abandon pets before listing some of the things that voluntary organisations can do if this happens.

Simplified activity: Ask the children to write down what might happen to animals that have been abandoned, e.g. they could die because of the cold or lack of food, or get run over.

Challenge: Ask the children to think about what voluntary organisations can do to tell people the right way to look after pets. For example, they could give talks, send out leaflets or advertise their services.

Worksheet 11 — The RSPCA

Starting points: Discuss what volunteers might do for this organisation, e.g. raise money, make visits to schools. Talk about the difference between someone who is employed by the charity and someone who is a volunteer.

Main activity: The children should design a poster advertising for people to join the RSPCA as volunteers.

Simplified activity: Ask the children to write down what might happen to animals if there were no organisations such as the RSPCA or the PDSA.

Challenge: The children could write a letter to a local newspaper asking people to support their local donkey sanctuary.

Worksheet 12 — Owning a pet

Starting points: Discuss who takes responsibility for pets at home. What does ownership of a pet mean? What happens if the owners go on holiday?

Main activity: The children should imagine that they are going on holiday and leaving their pet with a friend. They need to write down a list of things their friend must remember to do while the animal is being looked after.

Simplified activity: Ask the children what they would need if they were going to keep a cat or a pony. Which animal would be easier to look after? Explain why.

Challenge: The children could write a letter to a relative telling them what happened to their pet while they were away on holiday.

Plenary

Discuss what should be included in a book on pet care. Divide the class into groups and prepare some leaflets on the care of different pets.

PSHE & Citizenship in Action: Year 4

Worksheet 10

Unwanted pets

Make a list of some of the reasons why people abandon their pets.

1. _____
2. _____
3. _____
4. _____
5. _____
6. _____
7. _____
8. _____

What can voluntary organisations do to help these pets?

1. _____
2. _____
3. _____

How do the voluntary groups get money to feed the animals and look after them?

_____
_____
_____
_____

Worksheet 11

The RSPCA

 **Draw a poster advertising for people to join the RSPCA as volunteers.**

Worksheet 12

Owning a pet

 **Imagine you are going to leave your pet with a friend while you go on holiday. Write down what your friend will need to do to look after your pet.**

I am going away tomorrow for one week. Here is a list of what you will need, together with a timetable.

_____
_____
_____
_____
_____
_____
_____

Day	Timetable
Monday	
Tuesday	
Wednesday	
Thursday	
Friday	
Saturday	
Sunday	

5. The police

Background
It is important that children are aware of the impact of crime on the community. They need to be able to discuss the kind of problems they may face in their own area and also look at ways in which crime can be reduced.

Learning Objectives
Activities in this unit will allow children to:
- examine the kind of facilities that are available to young people in the area
- discuss vandalism and damage
- investigate antisocial behaviour.

QCA/Curriculum links: QCA Unit 4 • Worksheet 13 links with English, Maths, Design & Techology and Geography • Worksheet 14 links with English • Worksheet 15 links with English, Design & Technology and ICT.

ACTIVITIES

Worksheet 13 — What do we do?

Starting points: Talk about what kind of facilities are offered to young people in the area. What clubs are there? How old do you have to be to join? What is the benefit of being a member of certain clubs? Which clubs in the area support sports? Are there any national organisations such as the Scouts? Do any religious groups provide activities for young people, e.g. church, synagogue, mosque?

Main activity: The children should draw a map of the area marking the location of clubs suitable for young people. They should then find out the address of one club and the age of its members.

Simplified activity: Ask the children to mark the clubs on the map and write down what they are called.

Challenge: The children could find out the names and locations of clubs suitable for other age groups, e.g. young mothers, the elderly.

Worksheet 14 — Vandalism and damage

Starting points: Discuss why some young people damage other people's property. Talk about how this might affect someone, e.g. a young mother's car could be vandalised so that she cannot visit her sick father in hospital. Talk about the consequences of mindless vandalism. What can be done about it? Over 1000 telephone boxes are damaged every week. Discuss why this is a dangerous thing to do.

Main activity: The children should consider the situations on the worksheet. What would they do if they saw these things happening?

Simplified activity: The children could write down why they think it is wrong to damage other people's belongings.

Challenge: Ask the children to write down how they might work together with the police to reduce vandalism and damage in their area.

Worksheet 15 — Antisocial behaviour

Starting points: Look at some of the forms of antisocial behaviour, e.g. making a lot of noise late at night, dumping rubbish in open spaces, letting your dog foul the footpath, throwing things on to a railway line. Make a list of things that the children feel are unacceptable.

Main activity: The children should write a letter to the local police suggesting ways in which they might be able to reduce antisocial behaviour in their area.

Simplified activity: Ask the children to list some of the ways their area could be improved.

Challenge: The children could produce a set of leaflets to discourage antisocial behaviour.

Plenary
Conduct some role-play situations where someone is confronted after being antisocial. How can an individual or the local community stop this from happening? If the school is close to a railway line, invite a member of the British Transport Police to come in and talk about the dangers of throwing things on the line and trespassing.

PSHE & Citizenship in Action: Year 4

Worksheet 13

What do we do?

 **Draw a map of your area. Mark on it any clubs or organisations for young people.**

Name of club	Address	Age of members

Worksheet 14

Vandalism and damage

 What would you do if you saw these things happening?

Worksheet 15

Antisocial behaviour

 **Write a letter to the local police explaining what you think could be done to reduce antisocial behaviour in your area.**

 The world we live in

Background
Children need to understand that to survive we have to trade with other countries. There are some things that we are unable to produce which have to come from abroad. Also, some items may be cheaper if bought from other countries. These countries can be investigated and compared with their own. They should think about what it might be like to live in another country. How different would it be to where they live now?

Learning Objectives
Activities in this unit will allow children to:
- understand more fully the importance of trade with other countries
- look at ways in which countries work together
- consider life in a city elsewhere in the world.

QCA/Curriculum links: QCA Unit 5 • Worksheet 16 links with English, Maths and Geography • Worksheet 17 links with English, History and Geography • Worksheet 18 links with English, ICT and Geography.

ACTIVITIES

Worksheet 16 — International trade

Starting points: Ask the children to imagine that they live on a group of islands. Their own island only grows coconuts, but several other islands in the group grow other things. How might they start trading with other members of the group? Would they need to use money for trade?

Main activity: The children should look at the list of items and decide which are grown or made in the UK and which are made elsewhere. Which of these do we export and why?

Simplified activity: Ask the children to colour in green those things we export and red those items we import. Some things may be both green and red.

Challenge: The children should make a list of countries that supply us with different goods. How many things can they find that come from our nearest neighbours, e.g. France, the Netherlands, Belgium and Ireland?

Worksheet 17 — The global village

Starting points: Talk about the different ways countries might work together, e.g. conferences, sports events, art exhibitions, music. Investigate some of the major international sports events held around the world, e.g. the Olympic Games, the World Cup.

Main activity: The children should find out the answers to the questions on the Olympic Games.

Simplified activity: Ask the children to draw the Olympic flag. What does each ring represent?

Challenge: The children could create a new event for the Olympic Games. It should involve several sports and be suitable for male and female athletes.

Worksheet 18 — City life

Starting points: Show some pictures of cities around the world. Discuss how life might be different living in a city in another country. Talk about what things might differ.

Main activity: The children should choose one of the cities listed on the worksheet. Ask them to find out about it and write a diary for one day.

Simplified activity: Ask the children to locate each of these cities on a world map.

Challenge: The children could imagine what it might be like to move from one country to another. Ask them to write a short story about their first days in a new country.

Plenary
Discuss the possibility of starting up your own imaginary children's global television station. What kind of programmes would it have? Who would it be aimed at? Can you think of any problems, e.g. language, time differences?

Worksheet 16

International trade

Look at these items. Which are made or grown in the UK? Which are made or grown abroad?

	UK	Abroad
television	☐	☐
banana	☐	☐
CD	☐	☐
lemon	☐	☐

Which of the things that we grow or make in the UK do we send abroad (export)? Explain why.

_____
_____
_____
_____
_____

Worksheet 17

The global village

Answer these questions.

1. What is the Olympic Games?

2. How often is it held?

3. When and where will the next Summer Olympic Games be held?

4. What do the winners get as prizes?

5. When and where did the Olympic Games start?

6. Name three events from the Summer Olympic Games.

7. What takes place at the Winter Olympics?

8. What is carried to the opening ceremony?

9. How many rings are there on the Olympic flag?

10. Name two athletes who have won events at the Olympics.

11. Has the Olympic Games ever been held in the UK? If so, when?

12. What is a marathon?

13. What are 'field' events?

14. Name three countries that have hosted the Summer Olympic Games.

© Folens (copiable page) PSHE & Citizenship in Action: Year 4

Worksheet 18

City life

 **Choose *one* of these cities and find out something about it.**

> New York   Paris   Calcutta   Sydney
> Hong Kong   Tokyo

**Imagine you could spend a day in your chosen city.
Write a diary about your day.**

7.00 am _____
9.00 am _____
11.00 am _____
1.00 pm _____
3.00 pm _____
5.00 pm _____
7.00 pm _____
9.00 pm _____
11.00 pm _____

Draw a picture to show what happens at these times.

9.00 am	5.00 pm

Our school

Background
This unit provides children with the chance to work closely with others in the class and also those outside. It also allows them to communicate their views and devise a questionnaire which can be given to other children in the school. It also provides a chance for them to work together as a team.

Learning Objectives
Activities in this unit will allow children to:
- be part of a democratically elected committee
- learn to work together as a group
- develop a wide ranging questionnaire.

QCA/Curriculum links: QCA Unit 6 • Worksheet 19 links with English • Worksheet 20 links with English and PE • Worksheet 21 links with English, Science and Design & Technology.

ACTIVITIES

Worksheet 19 — Creating a committee

Starting points: Discuss what kind of improvements may be needed in the school grounds and talk about whether they are possible. Elect a committee to act on behalf of everyone in the class. The committee would be responsible for putting together possible plans, producing a timetable and co-ordinating the project.

Main activity: The children should make a list of the jobs that need to be carried out by the committee and then have a discussion on which are most important.

Simplified activity: Ask the children to write down five jobs that the committee should carry out.

Challenge: The children could consider what kind of sub-committees they would need, e.g. fund raising, publicity.

Worksheet 20 — Working together

Starting points: Discuss the improvement project with the children. Talk about how they might be able to involve people from outside. Make a list of people who might be helpful to their project. What kind of help might they require?

Main activity: The children should write a letter to someone who might be able to help them with their project.

Simplified activity: The children could make a list of people in and around the school who might be able to help.

Challenge: Ask the children to organise a meeting with someone who might be able to help. They could write a set of questions to be posed.

Worksheet 21 — What do you think?

Starting points: Discuss what the children intend to do in the playground. Prepare some plans and produce a set of questions to form the basis of a questionnaire that they can give to other children to see what they think.

Main activity: The children should draw a plan of the proposed alterations to the playground and then prepare a set of questions to find out what people think of them.

Simplified activity: Ask the children to draw a picture of their proposals.

Challenge: The children could make a model showing the proposal in detail. Put the model on display and ask for opinions.

Plenary
Talk about the importance of getting other people's points of view and opinions. These can then be used to change and modify the proposals. Discuss how important other people's ideas are. If they are going to use the equipment or area, they should be allowed some input into the discussion.

PSHE & Citizenship in Action: Year 4

Worksheet 19

Creating a committee

 **What kind of improvements may be needed in the school grounds? Fill in this worksheet about a committee that could be set up to carry out these changes.**

Name of committee _____

Jobs of the committee

_____
_____
_____
_____

Members of the committee

_____   _____
_____   _____
_____   _____
_____   _____

Possible sub-committees

_____   _____
_____   _____

Jobs of the sub-committees

_____
_____
_____
_____
_____
_____
_____

Worksheet 20

Working together

 **Write a letter to someone who might be able to help you with your project. Explain what you are going to do and ask what they might be able to do to help.**

Worksheet 21

What do you think?

Give this questionnaire to other children to find out what they think of your ideas.

Here are our ideas for the playground. We would like to know your opinions and ideas. Please answer the questions at the bottom. Use the back of this sheet for your answers.

Questions

_____
_____
_____
_____
_____
_____
_____
_____
_____
_____

© Folens (copiable page) PSHE & Citizenship in Action: Year 4

(8) Rights

Background
It is necessary for the children to understand that human beings should have rights. This unit gives them a chance to discuss what they feel are their basic rights, e.g. the right to a home, the right to be safe and secure. They will also have the opportunity to discuss what can be done if the rights they have are abused. This might also be the moment to play some trust games so that they can begin to realise that sometimes we need to trust other people.

Learning Objectives
Activities in this unit will allow children to:
- produce their own charter of rights
- decide what should be done if people's rights are abused
- discuss how situations of conflict can be resolved without force.

QCA/Curriculum links: QCA Unit 7 • Worksheet 22 links with English, Geography and Art & Design • Worksheet 23 links with English • Worksheet 24 links with English and Geography.

ACTIVITIES

Worksheet 22 — A charter of rights

Starting points: Discuss what kind of rights the children might have, e.g. the right to food and water, the right to learn, the right to choose their own friends. Split into groups and ask each group to come up with a list of five rights.

Main activity: The children should produce a charter of rights for children.

Simplified activity: Ask the children to discuss in their groups what their rights are as members of the class.

Challenge: The children could finalise the list of rights and decide on a title for them. Could these rights be adopted by children anywhere in the world?

Worksheet 23 — What happens if things go wrong?

Starting points: Discuss what could happen if any of the rights on the worksheet were abused. Talk about the possibility of forming a committee to consider cases where the children feel their rights have been abused.

Main activity: The children should look at the list on the worksheet and write down the ways in which these rights could be broken.

Simplified activity: Ask the children what they can do to see that the rights are kept to.

Challenge: The children could make a list of five problems that might be caused by the fact that sometimes everyone cannot have equal access to things, e.g. water fountains in the playground. How can this be sorted out?

Worksheet 24 — Sorting out conflict

Starting points: Talk about ways in which people might be able to resolve problems without violence. Discuss the importance of listening carefully to someone else's point of view and caring for other people's feelings.

Main activity: The children should suggest ways in which the countries on the worksheet might be able to sort out these problems peacefully.

Simplified activity: Ask the children to draw a peace poster.

Challenge: The children could consider what kind of people would be sent to sort out international problems. What qualities should they possess?

Plenary
Investigate the UN Convention on the Rights of the Child. How do these rights compare with their own charter?

Worksheet 22

A charter of rights

 Write your own charter of rights for children at your school.

Charter of rights

Worksheet 23

What happens if things go wrong?

 **Here is a list of children's rights. Write down how these rights might be broken.**

1. The right not to be bullied.

2. The right to food and water.

3. The right to make your own friends.

4. The right to feel safe.

5. The right to be able to learn in a quiet and safe place.

6. The right to play somewhere safe.

Worksheet 24

Sorting out conflict

**Read these problems.
What could be done to sort them out?**

1. Two countries, A and B, are arguing about their borders. Country A says that Country B has taken over its land.

   _____

   _____

2. Country A will not let people from Country B across its border.

   _____

   _____

3. Country A says that Country B has been sending its troops across the border looking for bandits without asking permission.

   _____

   _____

4. Country A has closed the road to the border because it says that people from Country B are crossing over without the right papers.

   _____

   _____

5. The prime minister of Country B says that the president of Country A was rude to him.

   _____

   _____

© Folens (copiable page) PSHE & Citizenship in Action: Year 4

(9) Rules and laws

Background
This unit looks at how it might be necessary to improve or change existing rules or laws if circumstances change. There is an opportunity for the children to revise the rules as well as look at specific laws relating to age. Finally, there is an opportunity to discuss the effects of a crime on a victim.

Learning Objectives
Activities in this unit will allow children to:
- learn that sometimes rules and laws have to be adapted
- find out more about laws relating to age
- investigate the effects on a victim of crime.

QCA/Curriculum links: QCA Unit 8 • Worksheet 25 links with English and Art & Design • Worksheet 26 links with English • Worksheet 27 links with English.

ACTIVITIES

Worksheet 25 — Improving rules

Starting points: What might happen in the school that would result in the rules being changed? Discuss some of the rules in the class and why these might need to be changed.

Main activity: The children should look at the list of rules and the changed circumstances and write down some new rules.

Simplified activity: Ask the children to draw a picture to go with each new rule.

Challenge: The children could investigate some of the rules of the road, e.g. speed. Why and how might these rules need to be changed?

Worksheet 26 — How old?

Starting points: Talk about laws that relate to age. These could include the minimum age at which you can marry, how old do you need to be to drive a motorbike, when you can go into a pub and buy a drink, and at what age you should have your own passport.

Main activity: The children should answer the questions on the sheet.

Simplified activity: Ask the children to draw a poster on the age you need to be to drive a car.

Challenge: Ask the children to imagine a country where there are no age limits for anything. What kind of problems might people face?

Worksheet 27 — Being the victim

Starting points: Talk about what it might be like to be the victim of a crime. Do the children know anyone who has been robbed or had their home burgled? If so, what was stolen and how did they feel? Set up some role-play situations where the police arrive at the scene of a crime for the first time.

Main activity: The children should write how they might feel in the situations on the worksheet.

Simplified activity: Ask the children to write down a slogan to prevent robbery and burglary.

Challenge: The children could make up their own 'help' organisation for victims of crime. What would it be called and what would they do to help the victims?

Plenary
Prepare an assembly on the theme of looking after your property. It should also deal with how people might feel after a crime.

Worksheet 25

Improving rules

Write down a new rule for each of these situations.

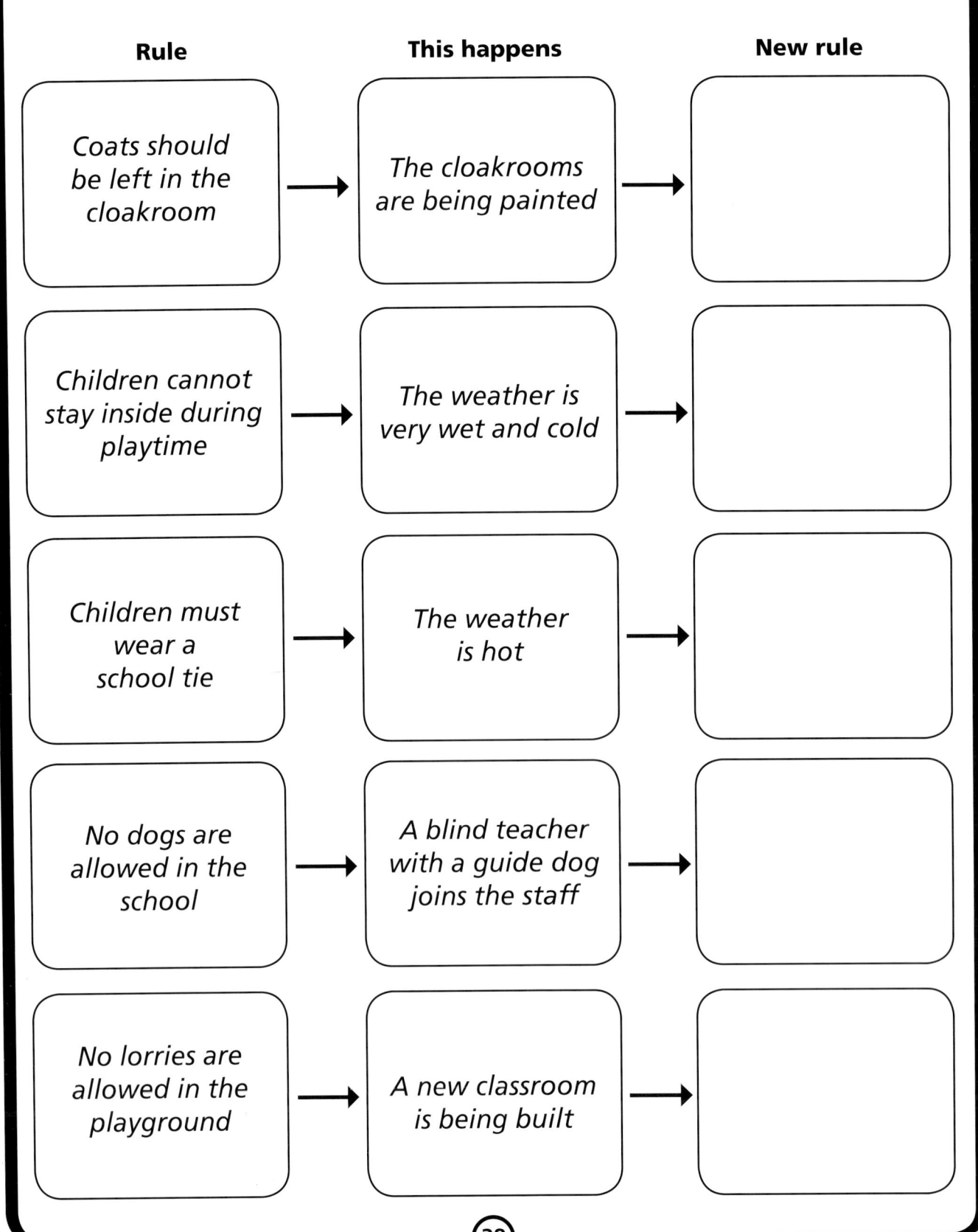

Rule	This happens	New rule
Coats should be left in the cloakroom	The cloakrooms are being painted	
Children cannot stay inside during playtime	The weather is very wet and cold	
Children must wear a school tie	The weather is hot	
No dogs are allowed in the school	A blind teacher with a guide dog joins the staff	
No lorries are allowed in the playground	A new classroom is being built	

© Folens (copiable page) PSHE & Citizenship in Action: Year 4

Worksheet 26

How old?

How old do you have to be to do each of these things?

1. Drive a motorbike (over 50cc) _____
2. Drive a car _____
3. Buy an alcoholic drink in a pub _____
4. Get married _____
5. Buy fireworks _____
6. Drive a moped (up to 50cc) _____
7. Drive a large tractor _____
8. Have a credit card _____

Why are children not allowed to buy alcohol?

_____

Why are people not allowed to buy fireworks under the age of 18?

_____

Write a story about introducing a new law which says how old you have to be before you can go into a supermarket on your own. Why has it been introduced? Does this law work?

_____
_____
_____
_____
_____
_____

Worksheet 27

Being the victim

Write down how you might feel if these things happened to you.

1. Your house is burgled.

2. You are hit over the head and your purse or wallet is stolen.

3. Someone smashes into your car and then drives away.

4. You are hit by someone for disagreeing with them.

5. Someone sprays paint all over your front door three nights in a row.

What would you say to the people who had done these things?

(10) Respect

Background
In this unit the children consider the act of shoplifting, why it is wrong and what might happen to someone if they were caught. They then deal with what measures can be put in place to stop shoplifting. Finally, they look at the importance of respecting school property.

Learning Objectives
Activities in this unit will allow children to:
- consider why it is wrong to steal from a shop
- think about what could be done to reduce shoplifting
- discuss how the irresponsible behaviour of a few can spoil the enjoyment of the majority.

QCA/Curriculum links: QCA Unit 9 • Worksheet 28 links with English and Art & Design • Worksheet 29 links with English, Science and Design & Technology • Worksheet 30 links with English and Maths.

ACTIVITIES

Worksheet 28 — Shoplifting

Starting points: Set up some role-play situations where a child is caught shoplifting. What happens to them? Discuss what might occur in a real-life situation. Is there any difference between stealing from a small shop and a large store?

Main activity: The children should draw a cartoon strip showing someone stealing from a store and then getting caught.

Simplified activity: Ask the children why a small shopkeeper is more at risk than the owner of a large store.

Challenge: The children could compile a questionnaire, to be handed out to small shopkeepers, on what might happen if someone is caught stealing in their shop.

Worksheet 29 — Making changes

Starting points: How can shopkeepers protect themselves against shoplifting? What can larger stores do to stop it from happening?

Main activity: The children should look at the two pictures on the worksheet. Ask them to write down what the shop and the store could do to deter shoplifters.

Simplified activity: Ask the children to draw on the pictures some of the ways in which the shop and the store could protect themselves, e.g. security cameras.

Challenge: The children could design an alarm system to stop people from stealing from shops.

Worksheet 30 — Respecting your school

Starting points: Why do some people want to damage schools? What can schools do to stop this from happening (e.g. fences, cameras, security locks)? Talk about why it is the right of everyone to enjoy the school and the grounds. What should happen to people if they are caught vandalising the school?

Main activity: The children should look at the school map, marking on any special security systems that could be used to deter vandals.

Simplified activity: Ask the children to make a list of the systems and devices that they have included on the map.

Challenge: The children could write a story about the day they caught someone breaking into their school.

Plenary
Look at a selection of alarm systems and discuss what each system does. Invite a local police officer to come to the school and ask them to talk about alarm systems and how effective they are.

Worksheet 28

Shoplifting

Draw a set of pictures showing someone stealing from a store and then being caught. Write what is happening in each picture in the space below each box.

1	2

3	4

5	6

42

© Folens (copiable page) PSHE & Citizenship in Action: Year 4

Worksheet 29

Making changes

☞ Look at these two pictures. What kind of things could the shop and the store do to stop shoplifting from taking place?

Small shop

Department store

43

© Folens (copiable page) PSHE & Citizenship in Action: Year 4

Worksheet 30

Respecting your school

☞ Look at this map of a school. Draw in some security systems that might stop vandals and burglars. Explain what they do.

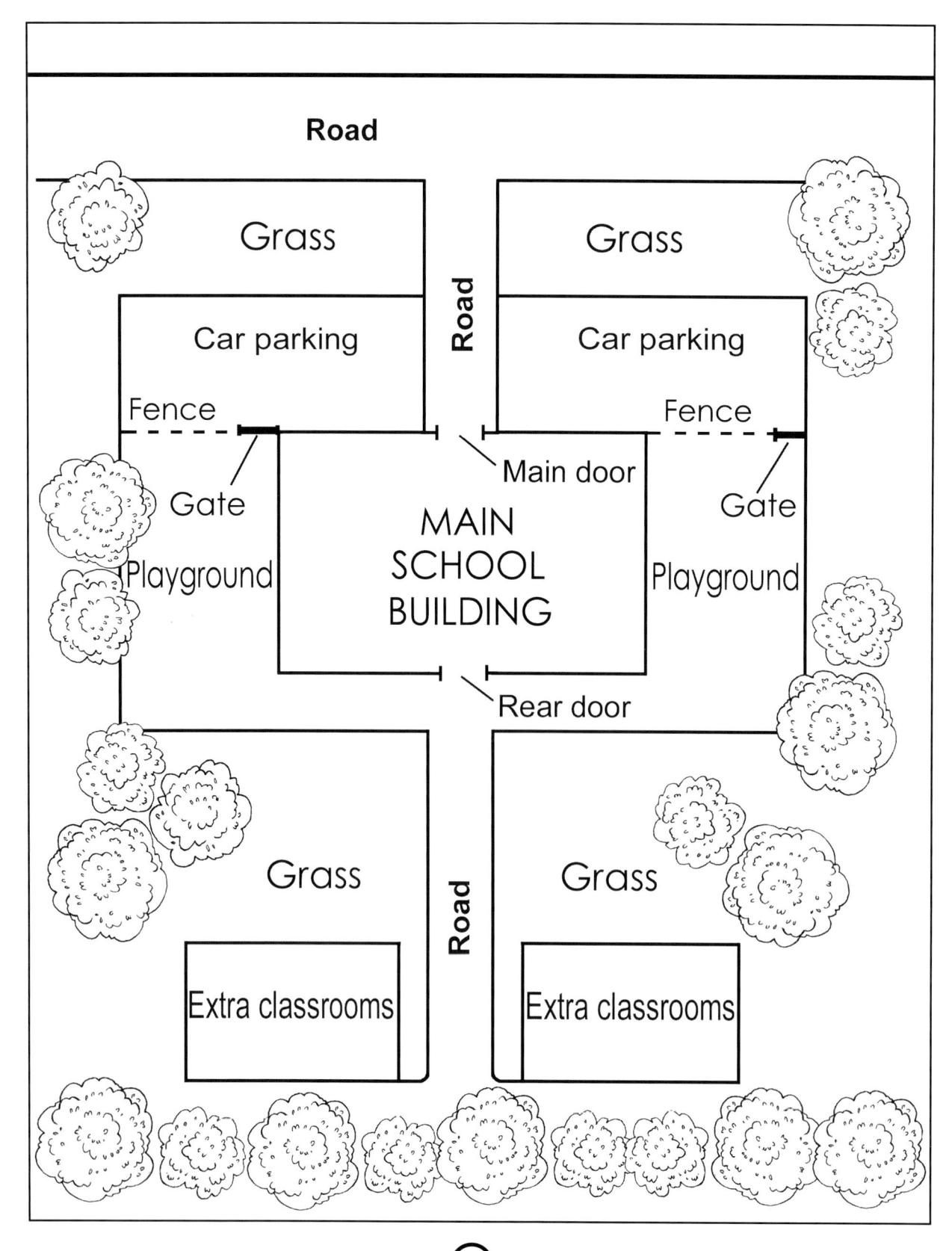

Road

Grass | Grass

Road

Car parking | Car parking

Fence | Fence

Gate | Main door | Gate

Playground | MAIN SCHOOL BUILDING | Playground

Rear door

Grass | Grass

Road

Extra classrooms | Extra classrooms

44

© Folens (copiable page) PSHE & Citizenship in Action: Year 4

(11) Local democracy

Background
This unit provides a chance to find out more about the local council and what they do. It also investigates how councillors are elected. What is the council tax used for and how is the money spent?

Learning Objectives
Activities in this unit will allow children to:
- explore the role of the local council
- find out more about their own parish or town council
- investigate how they are elected.

QCA/Curriculum links: QCA Unit 10 • Worksheet 31 links with English • Worksheet 32 links with English and Maths • Worksheet 33 links with English.

ACTIVITIES

Worksheet 31 — Our local council

Starting points: Look through a selection of local papers and magazines. Find and cut out any articles relating to the local council. Discuss what type of council is responsible for your area, e.g. parish, town, district. Where are their offices and how often do the local council meet?

Main activity: The children should find out who the local councillors are. Who is the chairperson of the council and the clerk? What is the address of the local council offices?

Simplified activity: Ask the children to draw the local council emblem.

Challenge: The children could imagine that they are attending a meeting of the local council. Write down three questions they could ask the councillors about their area.

Worksheet 32 — What do they do?

Starting points: Discuss what kind of things the local council might talk about at their meetings. What kind of jobs would they each have to do (e.g. planning, transport, schools)?

Main activity: The children should write down five questions that they would like to ask members of their local council. Imagine that they have been given £10,000 for the local area. How might they spend it?

Simplified activity: Ask the children to draw pictures of some of the local councillors who may have appeared in the local newspapers.

Challenge: The children could think about the idea that, if they were councillors, how would they spend the local council tax?

Worksheet 33 — Voting

Starting points: Discuss how you might run your own local election. You could find nine candidates who were willing to stand for election. These would have to say what they might be able to do for the local community.

Main activity: The children should write down how they might go about running their own local election. They could go on to produce a poster advertising the election.

Simplified activity: Ask the children to draw a picture of one of the candidates.

Challenge: The children could work out how they should organise the voting, e.g. secret ballot, vote for six candidates out of nine.

Plenary
Set up an imaginary council with six members, a chairperson and a clerk. Arrange a meeting when members of the class are allowed to ask questions. Get the clerk to record the meeting. Invite the local town or parish clerk in to talk about the role of the local council.

Worksheet 31

Our local council

Complete this worksheet about your local council.

Write down the address of your local council.

_____
_____
_____
_____
_____

Write down the names and jobs of the members of your local council.

Name	Job
_____	Chairperson
_____	Clerk
_____	_____
_____	_____
_____	_____
_____	_____
_____	_____
_____	_____
_____	_____
_____	_____

Worksheet 32

What do they do?

Write down five questions you would like to ask your local councillors about the local area.

1. _____
2. _____
3. _____
4. _____
5. _____

If you were given £10,000 to spend on the local area, how would you use it? Draw pictures of some of the things you would do.

Worksheet 33

Voting

If you were running your own local election:

1. Where would people vote?
_____

2. How many candidates would you allow?
_____

3. How many candidates would people be able to vote for?
_____

4. Who would you allow to vote?
_____

5. When would the election be?
_____

6. How would you get the ballot boxes containing the completed voting slips to a central place?
_____

7. How many staff would you have at each polling station?
_____

8. Who would be in charge of each polling station?
_____

9. Would you tell the police about the election? Explain why.
_____

10. When and where would you announce the winners?
_____

Draw a poster to advertise the election.

(12) The media

Background

We are constantly bombarded by news and other people's opinions. It is therefore vital that the children understand that news organisations select information to fit their audiences. The news also has to be sorted so that when a newspaper is published certain sections deal with certain issues, e.g. home news, sport, travel. Also, children may watch a number of soap operas on TV. These often use storylines to get over particular messages, which the children should be aware of.

Learning Objectives

Activities in this unit will allow children to:
- understand that the news can be directed to a specific audience by the use of headlines and style of writing
- find out more about how news is grouped under specific headings
- appreciate that television storylines often contain a message.

QCA/Curriculum links: QCA Unit 11 • Worksheet 34 links with English and ICT • Worksheet 35 links with English and ICT • Worksheet 36 links with English and Art & Design.

ACTIVITIES

Worksheet 34 — Headlines

Starting points: Look at a selection of newspapers and cut out some of the headlines. These could be used as a quiz, with the children guessing what stories they refer to. Talk about how the headlines are written so that they grab the reader's attention.

Main activity: The children should read the headlines and write a short article to go with them.

Simplified activity: Ask the children to look through a newspaper and cut out their favourite headlines or ones that stand out.

Challenge: The children could write a short report on something that has happened at school over the past week. Include a headline at the top of the piece.

Worksheet 35 — Sorting the news

Starting points: Discuss how different stories fit into different categories. Read out a selection of articles and ask the children to say which category they fall into, e.g. home news, foreign news, sport, travel, entertainment.

Main activity: The children should look at the headlines and sort them into the four categories.

Simplified activity: Ask the children to cut out some articles from a newspaper that are about sport, television and travel, sorting them into groups.

Challenge: The children could cut out a selection of articles from a newspaper and then decide on the top story for each section.

Worksheet 36 — Soap operas

Starting points: In small groups, ask the children to act out a scene from their favourite soap opera and get the others to guess the title. Talk about their favourite storylines and characters.

Main activity: The children should write a new scene for a current soap opera, using a storyline involving a lost child.

Simplified activity: Ask the children to list some favourite soap opera characters and say why they are popular.

Challenge: The children could list any problems or concerns that could be introduced into current soap opera storylines.

Plenary

Talk about what it might be like to work on a newspaper, television channel or radio station as a news reporter. Make up a new soap opera and introduce the characters in an assembly. Pick a theme for the scene, e.g. be careful on the roads, don't play near water.

Worksheet 34

Headlines

👉 Write a story to go with each of these newspaper headlines.

Chloe saves the day

Fire destroys famous home

Top prize goes to local school

Local lottery winner

Worksheet 35

Sorting the news

Sort these newspaper headlines under the correct headings.

- Dave scores early winning goal
- School closed because of cold weather
- New bus route to start
- Poppy gets gold medal
- Airport gets bigger
- Cheaper holidays to Spain
- Television show stars local girl
- Horse-riding champion visits town
- Larger screen for cinema
- Music event to be held in June

SPORT	HOME NEWS

TRAVEL	ENTERTAINMENT

Worksheet 36

Soap operas

Write a new scene for your favourite soap opera. It should be about a lost child.

_____
_____
_____
_____
_____
_____
_____
_____
_____
_____
_____
_____

Draw a picture of your scene.

13) At risk

Background
Children will have come into contact with different types of medicines over the years. Medicines are there to help fight disease and illness and make us better. This unit looks at why it is dangerous to take certain substances. Finally, it looks at the dangers of taking risks on the road.

Learning Objectives
Activities in this unit will allow children to:
- learn about safe, healthy routines
- discuss the dangers of taking certain substances
- understand that it is dangerous to take risks on the road.

QCA/Curriculum links: PSHE • Worksheet 37 links with English and Science • Worksheet 38 links with English, Science, Design & Technology and ICT • Worksheet 39 links with English.

ACTIVITIES

Worksheet 37 — Fighting illness

Starting points: Talk about how to prevent illness. Show some different safe medicines and ask what they might be used for. These could include cough mixture, painkillers, plasters, antibiotics and antiseptic cream.

Main activity: The children should match the sentences with the correct pictures.

Simplified activity: Ask the children to make a list of common illnesses.

Challenge: The children could design a poster to show one healthy routine.

Worksheet 38 — Taking a risk

Starting points: Talk about dangerous substances and how the containers could be made safer. Discuss why the substances may be dangerous.

Main activity: The children should colour in green the safe substances and red the dangerous ones.

Simplified activity: Ask the children to make up a simple safety song.

Challenge: The children could design a new form of container that can be opened only by an adult. They could write some instructions on how to use it.

Worksheet 39 — Safety on the road

Starting points: Explain to the children that they should never take risks on the road. Talk to the class about the importance of being safe and why they should never take a risk. Consider the consequences to the individual and other people.

Main activity: The children should consider the various situations on the worksheet, saying why each one is dangerous and what might happen.

Simplified activity: Ask the children to write a short story about someone who took a risk and was hurt because of it.

Challenge: The children could produce a sign to be put up in their area telling people that it is dangerous to take risks.

Plenary
Ask a nurse from your local clinic or hospital to come and explain the kind of injuries that might occur if the children take risks.

Worksheet 37

Fighting illness

Match these sentences with the right picture. Write the picture number next to the sentence.

Wash your hands after going to the toilet. _____

Use a handkerchief when you sneeze. _____

Wash your hands before you eat. _____

Brush your hair regularly. _____

If you cut yourself, clean the wound and put some antiseptic cream or a plaster on it. _____

Clean your teeth at least twice a day. _____

1   2   3

4   5   6

Worksheet 38

Taking a risk

Look at the things below. Colour in red the dangerous things and green the safe things.

- Bleach
- GLUE
- Coffee
- Milk
- Hairspray
- Weedkiller
- Orange Juice
- Petrol
- White Paint
- Lemonade

How could you make the containers safer?

_____
_____

55

© Folens (copiable page) PSHE & Citizenship in Action: Year 4

Worksheet 39

Safety on the road

Why are these things dangerous to do?

1. Ride your bike at night without lights.

2. Walk along an unlit road in dark clothes at night.

3. Drive over the 30 mph speed limit.

4. Run across the road.

5. Overtake on a bend.

6. Travel in a car without wearing a seatbelt.

7. Play football in the road.

8. Use a mobile phone when driving.

14 Drugs

Background
This unit looks at why people take drugs, and the dangers of smoking and alcohol. Children may know people who take drugs or have contact with those who have done so in the past. They need to consider the facts about smoking and alcohol and what they do to the body.

Learning Objectives
Activities in this unit will allow children to:
- learn more about the dangers of drugs
- understand what smoking does to the body
- consider how alcohol can affect the way people behave.

QCA/Curriculum links: PSHE • Worksheet 40 links with English and Science • Worksheet 41 links with English and Science • Worksheet 42 links with English, Science and Art & Design.

ACTIVITIES

Worksheet 40 — Why take drugs?

Starting points: Discuss why some young people take drugs. What are they hoping to get from the experience? Discuss why most people do not take drugs.

Main activity: The children should complete the sentences on the worksheet and write down some reasons why young people might take drugs.

Simplified activity: Ask the children to make up a short play about a child who is given medicines to help them overcome illness.

Challenge: The children could write a story about a drug that helped someone get better.

Worksheet 41 — Smoking

Starting points: Ask the children if they know anyone who smokes. Do they smoke a lot? When do they smoke? Have they ever thought of stopping? What do they think is happening to their body?

Main activity: The children should draw an anti-smoking poster in the space provided on the worksheet.

Simplified activity: Ask the children to list words linked to smoking.

Challenge: The children could find out more about the dangers of smoking by going to www.ash.org.uk. They could then produce their own leaflet explaining the dangers.

Worksheet 42 — The dangers of alcohol

Starting points: Talk about what happens if someone drinks too much alcohol. How does the body change? Make a list of favourite non-alcoholic drinks. Discuss why adults do not allow children to drink alcohol.

Main activity: The children should write a story about someone who is affected by alcohol.

Simplified activity: Ask the children to draw a selection of pub signs.

Challenge: The children could carry out a survey to find out what kind of alcohol is drunk at home. They could draw charts and graphs to show their results.

Plenary
You may want to produce an assembly on one of these topics, concentrating on the dangers of smoking or alcohol. Carry out a survey to find out how many children think smoking and drinking alcohol is a bad idea. Display the results to the rest of the school in the form of charts, graphs or a presentation.

Worksheet 40

Why take drugs?

Using the words in brackets, complete these sentences on why some people take drugs. Underline the three most important reasons.

I like to feel _____ (cool, clever, warm)

I want to forget _____ (everything, my name, school)

I want to fit in with my _____ (school, gang, home)

I do it for _____ (money, my parents, fun)

I cannot say _____ (yes, no, help)

I want to know what it feels _____ (about, like, inside)

For what other reasons do some people take drugs?

_____
_____
_____
_____
_____
_____
_____
_____
_____
_____
_____

Worksheet 41

Smoking

Draw an anti-smoking poster.

Worksheet 42

The dangers of alcohol

Write a story about someone who is affected by alcohol.

(15) Bullying

Background
This unit builds on the previous work undertaken on bullying. It looks at the importance of being different and confident when facing a bully. It also investigates ways in which the children can fight against bullying.

Learning Objectives
Activities in this unit will allow children to:
- understand the importance of being different
- increase their confidence
- investigate further ways of dealing with bullies.

QCA/Curriculum links: PSHE • Worksheet 43 links with English and History • Worksheet 44 links with English and Music • Worksheet 45 links with English.

ACTIVITIES

Worksheet 43 Being different

Starting points: Children sometimes get picked on because they are different. It is important to stress the importance of being an individual. Ask the children what makes them special and different from anyone else.

Main activity: The children should look at the pictures on the worksheet and write down what makes each person special. Why are they unique?

Simplified activity: Ask the children to think of a friend. Why are they different? What are they good at? What makes them special?

Challenge: The children could investigate a few famous people in history. What made them different?

Worksheet 44 Being confident

Starting points: Bullies often pick on people who are vulnerable. It is important that children are confident in their attitude and the way they behave. This will often deter bullies from picking on them.

Main activity: The children should write down a list of things they are good at before completing the sentences.

Simplified activity: Ask the children to make up a song about being special.

Challenge: Ask the children to write a list of qualities that are needed to make a person happy.

Worksheet 45 Beating the bully

Starting points: Talk about ways in which the children might be able to stop a bully (a) when they are in a group, and (b) when they are on their own.

Main activity: The children should look at the ways in which they could fight a bully, ticking those they consider the most important. They could then go on to write a poem about bullying.

Simplified activity: Ask the children to draw a cartoon strip showing how one person managed to beat a bully.

Challenge: The children could write a short story about what it might be like to be a bully.

Plenary
Introduce a campaign in your school to stop bullying. Encourage children to have more fun at playtime and introduce new games.

Worksheet 43

Being different

What makes these people special? Why are they unique?

Worksheet 44

Being confident

Fill in this worksheet.

I am good at _____

_____

_____

Complete these sentences using the words in the boxes.

If you come across a bully you must:

1. Know what _____

2. Be able to deal with _____

3. Know when to say _____

4. Like _____

5. Feel _____

| angry people | who you are |

| is important |

| good about yourself | no! |

Worksheet 45

Beating the bully

Tick the sentences you think are the most important.

To fight against bullies you need to be:

1. Good looking. ☐
2. Able to stay in a group. ☐
3. Able to ask for help. ☐
4. Very strong. ☐
5. Ready to keep a diary. ☐
6. Good at your answers. ☐
7. In sight of an adult. ☐
8. Ready to fight. ☐
9. Able to keep calm. ☐
10. Happy about who you are. ☐

Write a poem called 'Beating the Bully'.

_____
_____
_____
_____
_____
_____
_____
_____